STEAM IN THE EAST MIDLANDS AND EAST ANGLIA

ABOUT THE PHOTOGRAPHER

R.J. (Ron) Buckley was born in 1917, and after the family moved to a house overlooking Spring Road station, near Tyseley, in 1926 his interest in railways grew. After joining the Birmingham Locomotive Club in 1932, he made frequent trips with them throughout the country, also accompanying W.A. Camwell on his many branch line tours. From 1936 until 1939 these club tours included visits to the East Midland counties and East Anglia where he photographed many examples of the pre-grouping locomotive classes still working with both the LNER and the LM&SR.

In 1934 he joined the LM&SR as a wages clerk at Lawley Street goods station, Birmingham, and after the declaration of war in September 1939 he was called up and joined the Royal Engineers, being posted to the No. 4 Dock Operating Unit. Serving briefly in Norway during March 1940, he was by May of that year with a special party supplying stores for the returning troops at Dunkirk. Ron was evacuated from Dunkirk on the *Maid of Orleans*, an ex-Southern Railway cross-channel ferry, and by 1941 he was in Egypt with his unit supporting the 8th Army in its advance from Alamein finally reaching Tripoli. In 1944 his unit was in Alexandria before returning to Britain during 1945 and being demobbed in May 1946.

His employment with the LM&SR continued; he was based at Kings Heath in Birmingham and at Derby in the British Railways Divisional Managers Office from 1948. His job at Derby saw his duties take him out of the office, visiting sites to attend meetings, which enabled him to take photographs at many distant locations. He was also a spectator of the continual stream of locomotives passing through the works at Derby, and photographed many of the new British Railway Standard locomotives constructed there. Further organised visits to East Anglia and the East Midlands from 1946 to 1949 and throughout the 1950s and 1960s gave him the opportunity to witness the changes that had taken place in locomotive power in the counties comprising the East Midlands and East Anglia.

Married in 1948 to Joyce, the daughter of an LNER locomotive driver, Ron retired in 1977 after over forty-two years' service with the railways. He and his wife currently live in Staffordshire.

STEAM IN THE EAST MIDLANDS AND EAST ANGLIA

THE RAILWAY PHOTOGRAPHS OF R.J. (RON) BUCKLEY

COMPILED BY BRIAN J. DICKSON

The
History
Press

Other books in this series:

Steam in Scotland: *The Railway Photographs of R.J. (Ron) Buckley*
Southern Steam: *The Railway Photographs of R.J. (Ron) Buckley*
Steam in the North East: *The Railway Photographs of R.J. (Ron) Buckley*
Great Western Steam: *The Railway Photographs of R.J. (Ron) Buckley*
COMING SOON: *London Midland Steam*: *The Railway Photographs of R.J. (Ron) Buckley*

First published 2018

The History Press
The Mill, Brimscombe Port
Stroud, Gloucestershire, GL5 2QG
www.thehistorypress.co.uk

British Library Cataloguing in Publication Data.
A catalogue record for this book is available from the British Library.

ISBN 978 0 7509 8439 3

Typesetting and origination by The History Press
Printed in Great Britain

Front cover: Saturday 24 May 1952. Ex-GER Class D56 (LNER Class D16) 4-4-0 No. 62577, bearing a 32A – Norwich shed code, is waiting to depart from Wells-on-Sea with the 1.35 p.m. working to Heacham. This branch of the GER would be closed a week later, at the end of May.

Back cover: Saturday 3 July 1954. The Stephenson Locomotive Society Midland Area Branch's Derby and Nottingham Rail Tour from Derby to Nottingham had reached Mansfield Midland station with Class 2MT 2-6-0 No. 46443 at its head. Seen here during the photographic stop taking water, she was the product of Crewe Works during 1949 that would be withdrawn in 1967. Bought and entering the preservation scene, she is currently awaiting an overhaul at the Severn Valley Railway.

Half-title page: Sunday 10 April 1960. Edward Thompson planned to rebuild the Nigel Gresley-designed three-cylinder Class K4 2-6-0s into a two-cylinder variety, but only one locomotive was so treated. With Arthur Peppercorn in the CME's chair from 1946, he oversaw a number of modifications to Thompson's proposal and the result was the Class K1 locomotives with a total of seventy examples being constructed by the NBL during 1949 and 1950. Seen here at March shed is No. 62040. Constructed in 1949, she would be withdrawn from service during 1965.

Title page: Saturday 18 April 1959. Edward Thompson had also planned for the rebuilding of Nigel Gresley's three-cylinder Class B17 4-6-0 locomotives into a two-cylinder variation incorporating a new boiler to be classified B2. Only ten examples were so rebuilt, including No. 61616 *Falladon* seen here at Stratford shed yard. Originally constructed as Class B17 No. 2816 at Darlington Works in 1930, she would be rebuilt during 1945. With only a few months of her working life remaining, she would be withdrawn later in 1959.

INTRODUCTION

This volume of photographs from Ron Buckley's collection follows his perambulations throughout the eastern shires of England, encompassing the counties of Lincoln, Cambridge, Nottingham, Rutland, Leicester, Northampton, Norfolk and Suffolk. Included in this volume are the counties of Bedford, Hertford, Buckingham and Essex, which fit neatly into the compass of this volume.

East Anglia, with its rich agricultural countryside, was primarily ex-Great Eastern Railway territory with its main lines reaching north to Cambridge and Peterborough and north-east to Colchester, Ipswich and Norwich. It also served the coastal towns of Lowestoft, Yarmouth and Cromer, whose fishing fleets contributed huge amounts of traffic for the railway, and to Kings Lynn, Wisbech and Wells-on-Sea with their busy harbours. The company had also invested heavily in the infrastructure at Parkeston Quay and Harwich, which became important in supporting the ferry services they operated to continental Europe, later to be inherited by the LNER and British Railways. The many rural branch lines may not have shown much passenger revenue, but they were crucial for carrying agricultural produce out of the region. The LNER inherited many excellent locomotive classes from the GER such as the reliable 'Claud Hamilton' 4-4-0s and the large B16 4-6-0s, both of which were at one time responsible for handling the heavy passenger traffic on the Norwich route out of Liverpool Street. The LNER itself introduced the Nigel Gresley-designed three-cylinder Class B17 4-6-0s to work this route, and under British Railways this

route saw the introduction of the Standard 'Britannia' class of 4-6-2s. Goods traffic was primarily in the hands of the Class J15 0-6-0s, examples of which were allocated to sheds throughout the old GER territory, while heavier goods traffic was often handled by the powerful Class J16 and J17 0-6-0s. Suburban traffic operating out of London Liverpool Street was allocated to a series of very able tank locomotives that culminated in the reliable Alfred Hill-designed Class L77 (LNER Class N7) 0-6-2 tanks.

The only interloper in the north of East Anglia was the Midland & Great Northern Joint Railway (M&GNJR), jointly owned by the Midland and the Great Northern Railways which would, after the grouping have as its owners the LMS and the LNER. With its long, mostly single-track route from Peterborough and Spalding to Norwich, Yarmouth and Cromer, it was able to tap into the agricultural traffic, with its other source of revenue being the carriage of coal from the Nottinghamshire coalfield to the cities and towns it served. Becoming solely operated by the LNER from 1936, its locomotive fleet consisted mainly of Midland Railway-designed 0-6-0s with some LNER 4-4-0s operating the passenger services. Post-nationalisation, the use of ex-LMS classes became normal practice, with the Henry George Ivatt-designed Class 4MT 2-6-0s handling much of the traffic up until the closure of the route in 1959.

In the south of the region, the London, Tilbury & Southend Railway (LT&SR) sourced its revenue from both the commuter traffic into London Fenchurch Street and the goods traffic being handled through the docks at Tilbury. From 1916 until the early 1960s this port was handling cruise liner traffic together with the many ships carrying emigrants from the United Kingdom to Australia, the so called 'ten-pound pom boats'. The railway, being well placed to handle this traffic, often organised special boat trains.

With its main line running north from London Kings Cross through Peterborough and Grantham to Doncaster, the ex-Great Northern Railway sphere of influence extended to much of Lincolnshire, with long branches reaching through Boston to Mablethorpe, Skegness, Horncastle and Grimsby – the northern part of the county being almost entirely ex-Great Central Railway territory. The GCR had become a huge investor in the growth of Grimsby Docks, supplying the rail connections to tap into the large quantities of fish traffic generated. During much of the LNER period and into the early British Railways reign many of these Lincolnshire branches were worked by Class C12 4-4-2 tanks, often in push-pull mode. Much of the East Coast Main Line traffic between London and Scotland was in the hands of the Class A3 Pacifics until September 1935 when Nigel Gresley's Class A4s, which were destined to haul the 'Silver Jubilee', were introduced. Further examples of the class followed from Doncaster Works from 1936, with a total of thirty-five class members entering service by 1938. These found much use on the named expresses such as the 'Coronation' service to Edinburgh from 1937, the 'Capitals Limited' and the 'Flying Scotsman'. During the post-nationalisation period, the Arthur Peppercorn-designed Class A1 Pacifics were also widely used for East Coast passenger traffic. The LNER had inherited a huge number of six-coupled goods locomotives from the Great Northern, Great Central and Great Eastern Railways, classified J1 to J20, which it continued to use well into the late 1940s, with many examples seeing out their working lives under British Railway ownership. Ron was fortunate to be able to photograph a few of the remaining ex-GCR locomotive classes still working both prior to and after nationalisation.

Many of the larger John Robinson-designed classes introduced during the early part of the twentieth century had been withdrawn before nationalisation. The most prominent exceptions were the very reliable Class 8K (LNER Class O4) 2-8-0s, of which many hundreds had been constructed both for the GCR and the ROD. Used for heavy goods and mineral traffic, these locomotives continued in traffic, with many giving over fifty years of service before they were withdrawn during the mid 1960s.

In contrast to the agricultural riches of East Anglia, the county of Nottinghamshire had a long history of coal mining, with large numbers of mines sunk north of Nottingham and in the Dukeries area. Needless to say, railways vied to carry this rich traffic, with both the Midland Railway and the Great Central Railway being heavily involved with the Nottingham coalfields. To handle this traffic the Midland Railway produced a series of very reliable 0-6-0s, which were designed by Matthew Kirtley and Samuel Johnson. The final 0-6-0s, designed by Henry Fowler, were unfortunately prone to mechanical failures. For express passenger work the Midland Railway's dependence on the 4-4-0 wheel arrangement continued until after the grouping, when the LMS introduced a series of powerful three-cylinder 4-6-0s, with the 'Royal Scot' Class entering service during 1927. It was not until after the William Stanier-designed 'Princes Royal' Class Pacifics were introduced in 1933, followed by his 'Princess Coronation' Class in 1937, that many of the former MR and LMS 'Compound' and '2P' 4-4-0s were relegated to secondary work.

Ron Buckley's photographs show the changes in the locomotive scene that took place throughout these two areas, illustrating from the later 1930s those pre-grouping classes still working and the newer classes being introduced by both the LMS and the LNER. Ron's later photographs, from 1946 onwards, show more of these remaining working pre-grouping locomotives and additionally portray the newer designs of Edward Thompson and Arthur Peppercorn.

Sunday 10 May 1936. Standing in Retford Great Northern shed yard is ex-GCR Class 9J (LNER Class J11) 0-6-0 No. 5980. Constructed by Neilson Reid & Co. during 1901, with a saturated boiler, she would be rebuilt in 1937 with a superheated boiler, be renumbered 4287 by the LNER in 1946, be numbered 64287 by British Railways and finally be withdrawn during 1959. The class, designed by John Robinson, consisted of 170 examples, which were built by a variety of manufacturers: Gorton Works, Neilson Reid & Co., Beyer Peacock & Co., the Vulcan Foundry and the Yorkshire Engine Co.

Sunday 10 May 1936. This powerful locomotive was from a design by John Robinson. Ex-GCR Class 8K (LNER Class O4) 2-8-0 No. 6230 was built during 1912 by the NBL. Seen here at Retford Great Northern shed, she was destined to be loaned and finally sold to the War Department during the early 1940s, shipped to the Middle East and never to return to the UK.

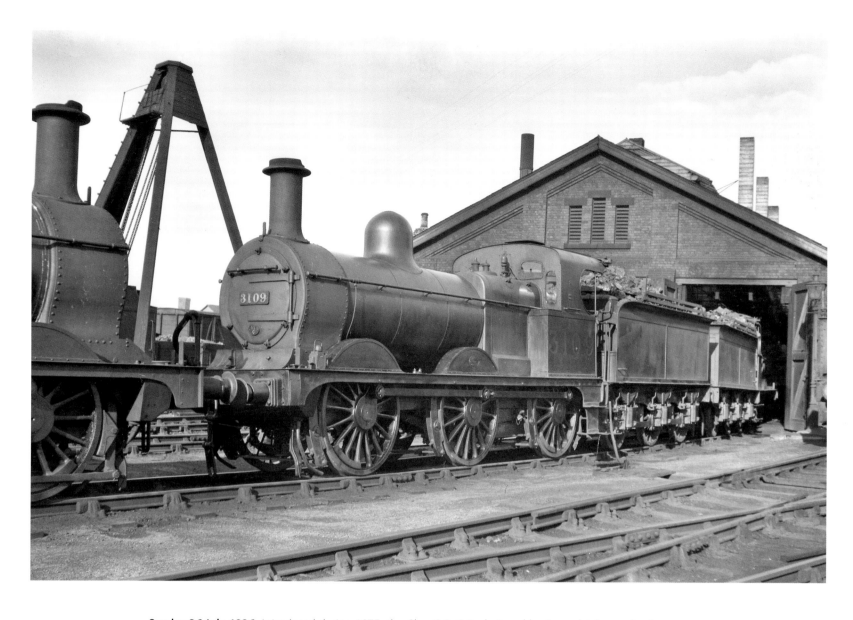

Sunday 26 July 1936. Introduced during 1875, the Class 2 0-6-0s designed by Samuel Johnson for the Midland Railway continued construction up to 1902, with many outside contractors delivering large numbers. Seen here at Coalville shed and bearing the correct 17C shed code is No. 3109, which was produced by Beyer Peacock & Co. during 1883. Originally numbered 1611 by the MR, she would be withdrawn from service in 1949.

Sunday 4 July 1937. The first of John Robinson's design of Atlantic locomotives for the GCR was his Class 8B, introduced in 1903, with a total of twenty-seven examples being constructed up to 1906 and being classified C4 by the LNER. Seen here at Woodford Halse shed is No. 6085, built by the NBL during 1905. She would receive a superheating boiler in 1925 and be withdrawn from service during 1950.

Sunday 4 July 1937. With 6ft 9in driving wheels, this impressive locomotive is one of only a pair constructed to a design by John Robinson for the GCR express passenger services. Seen here at Woodford Halse shed, ex-GCR Class 8C (LNER Class B1, later B18) 4-6-0 No. 5195 was constructed by Beyer Peacock & Co. during 1903 and would be withdrawn at the end of 1947.

Sunday 4 July 1937. Seen at Woodford Halse shed are two examples of ex-GCR Class 9Q (LNER Class B7) 4-6-0s. This four-cylinder class was primarily designed for mixed traffic work, with a total of thirty-eight examples being constructed between 1921 and 1924. Twenty-three of the class came from Gorton Works, ten from the Vulcan Foundry and five from Beyer Peacock & Co. *Top*: No. 5036 was a Vulcan Foundry example from 1921 that would be withdrawn during 1948 and *Bottom*: No. 5073 was a Gorton Works product, also from 1921, which would be withdrawn in 1949.

Sunday 5 September 1937. Seen standing in New England shed yard, Peterborough, is LNER Class K3 2-6-0
No. 158. This class of three-cylinder locomotives, designed by Nigel Gresley, was introduced during 1920
as GNR Class H4. A total of 193 were constructed up to 1937. No. 158 was a product of Darlington Works
during 1925. Numbered 61847 by British Railways, it would be withdrawn in 1962.

Sunday 5 September 1937. The graceful lines of the Thomas Worsdell design of Class Y14 0-6-0 for the GER are clearly seen here. They were introduced during 1883 and construction continued until 1913; over 280 entered service. The majority were built at Stratford Works, with a few coming from Sharp Stewart & Co. during 1884. Classified J15 by the LNER and known by some Great Eastern crews as 'Little Goods', these versatile locomotives were to be found allocated and working all over the old Great Eastern territory. No. 7854 is seen here in New England shed yard. She was built at Stratford Works in 1889 and would be numbered 65372 by British Railways and withdrawn during 1949.

Sunday 26 September 1937. Seen here in Peterborough East shed yard is an example of the James Holden-designed Class F48 0-6-0 goods locomotive for the GER. No. 8202 was constructed at Stratford Works during 1902 with a round-top firebox. She would be rebuilt during 1922 with a Belpaire firebox and superheated boiler, as seen here. Becoming Class J17 with the LNER, she would be numbered 65552 by British Railways and withdrawn by them in 1955.

Sunday 26 September 1937. Seen here in Kings Cross shed yard is what is generally considered to be Nigel Gresley's masterpiece class of express passenger locomotive design. Introduced during 1935 to operate the 'Silver Jubilee' service between London and Newcastle, Class A4 No. 2510 *Quicksilver* is seen in its original grey livery. All thirty-five locomotives in this class were constructed at Doncaster Works, and *Quicksilver* was the second to enter service. She spent much of her working life allocated to Kings Cross, and was withdrawn in 1963.

Saturday 12 March 1938. Much has been written about the history of LNER No. 4472 *Flying Scotsman*. Designed by Nigel Gresley and constructed during 1923 at Doncaster Works as a Class A1 locomotive, she would be rebuilt as a Class A3 during 1947 and withdrawn after forty years of service in 1963. Purchased privately and subsequently coming into the National Collection, after a major rebuild she came back into service in 2016. She is seen here in glistening condition at Kings Cross shed.

Saturday 12 March 1938. *Above*: Having just propelled a string of coal wagons up the ramp and into the coaling stage at Bletchley shed, ex-LNWR Class 18" 'Passenger' (LMS Class 2P) 0-6-2 tank No. 6900 is waiting to be uncoupled from its load. Constructed at Crewe Works to a design by Francis Webb during 1889, she would be the last member of her class to be withdrawn by British Railways in 1953. *Opposite, top*: The 'Prince of Wales' Class of two-cylinder 4-6-0s, designed by Charles Bowen-Cooke for express passenger traffic on the LNWR, entered service during 1911, with a total of 246 examples being constructed. No. 25694, bearing its LMS duplicate list number, is seen here at Bletchley shed bearing a 2C Northampton shed code. A product of Crewe Works during 1919, she would be withdrawn in 1947. *Opposite, bottom*: Classified 3P by the LMS, the 'Prince of Wales' locomotives were constructed in batches by Crewe Works, William Beardmore & Co. and the NBL. No. 25791 is seen here at Bletchley station. Built by William Beardmore & Co. during 1921, she would be withdrawn in 1947.

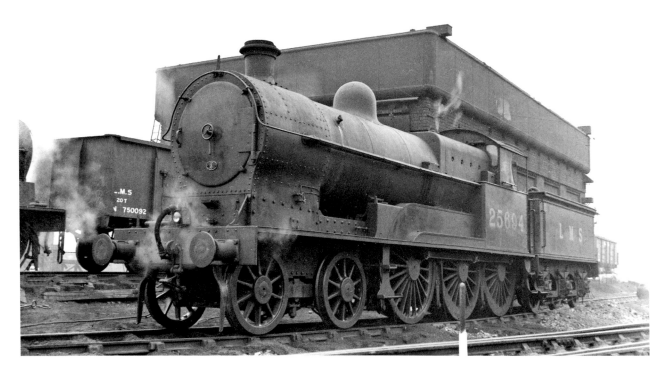

Saturday 12 March 1938. Designer James Holden's 'Claud Hamilton' class of 4-4-0s were introduced during 1900, with the final variation of the design entering service post-grouping in 1923. Ex-GER Classes S46, D56 and H88 were reclassified D14, D15 and D16 by the LNER, with many examples being rebuilt over a period of years with superheating boilers and Belpaire fireboxes. Seen here in Stratford shed yard is No. 8781, which was constructed at Stratford Works during 1923 as a Class D16. She would be withdrawn in 1959, numbered 62612.

Saturday 12 March 1938. Photographed in sparkling ex-works condition in Stratford Works yard is ex-M&GNJR Class D (LNER Class J41) 0-6-0 No. 069. Constructed by Kitson & Co. during 1899, using a Samuel Johnson Midland Railway design, she was part of a class of sixteen locomotives purchased by the M&GNJR – eight from Neilson Reid & Co. during 1896 and eight from Kitson & Co. in 1899. Allocated to Yarmouth Beach shed, she would be withdrawn during 1942.

Saturday 12 March 1938. Thomas Worsdell introduced the 2-4-2 tank wheel arrangement to the GER during 1884 with his Class M15 (LNER Class F4), construction continuing until 1909. They turned out to be heavy users of coal and were not very successful. No. 7111, seen here in Stratford shed yard, was constructed during 1907 and fitted with condensing gear, which was later removed. Loaned to the War Department between 1941 and 1945 for coastal defence work, she would be withdrawn in 1948.

Sunday 13 March 1938. The design of this double-framed locomotive is the work of Matthew Kirtley for the Midland Railway. Ex-MR Class '700' (LMS Class 2F) 0-6-0 No. 22846 bears its LMS duplicate list number. Over 300 examples were constructed in total, by Derby Works and a number of outside suppliers, including Dübs & Co., Kitson & Co., Neilson Reid & Co., the Vulcan Foundry and John Fowler Ltd. The example seen here at Nottingham shed was a product of Dübs & Co. during 1873, numbered 1044 by the MR. She would become No. 58111 with British Railways and would finally be withdrawn after seventy-six years of service in 1949.

Sunday 10 April 1938. The steam locomotives in the ownership of the Metropolitan Railway were acquired by the LNER during November 1937, with that company becoming responsible for the operation of passenger and goods traffic north of Rickmansworth. Designed by the Metropolitan Railway CME Charles Jones, the eight examples of his Class H (LNER Class H2) 4-4-4 tanks were constructed by Kerr Stuart & Co. and delivered during 1920 and 1921. With relatively short working lives, all eight examples ended their days in Nottinghamshire. Seen here in plain black livery shortly after her acquisition, standing in Stratford shed yard, is No. 6418, built in 1920. She would be withdrawn after only twenty-six years of service in 1946.

Sunday 6 August 1939. Parked adjacent to Leicester Great Central shed is ex-GNR Class J23 (LNER Class J50) 0-6-0 tank No. 3213. One of Nigel Gresley's earlier designs, introduced during 1914, she was originally constructed at Doncaster Works during 1919 and would give forty years' service before being withdrawn in 1959, then numbered 68912.

Sunday 28 April 1946. The locomotive seen here in Nottingham shed yard is already 80 years old having been constructed at Derby Works during 1866. Designed by Matthew Kirtley for the Midland Railway to haul express passenger traffic, No. 20002 was originally numbered 158A by them and spent the last couple of years working as station pilot at Nottingham. Withdrawn during 1947, she was restored for display purposes and finally became part of the National Collection. She can now be seen in all her restored glory at the Midland Railway Centre at Butterley.

Thursday 22 August 1946. Seen here in the yard at Yarmouth Beach shed is ex-GER Class S56 (LNER Class J69) 0-6-0 tank No. 7082. Constructed at Stratford Works in 1904 to a design by James Holden, they were primarily utilised on suburban passenger duties. Most of the class ended their days on shunting or station pilot work, with No. 7082 becoming No. 68268 with British Railways and being withdrawn in 1958.

Thursday 22 August 1946. Originally designed for the GCR passenger traffic between Manchester and Altringham, ex-GCR Class 9G (LNER Class F2) 2-4-2 tank No. 7112 is a long way from its origins here at Yarmouth South station. The class of ten examples were designed by Harry Pollitt and constructed by Beyer Peacock & Co. during 1898. During the 1940s a number of the class were transferred to East Anglia for passenger duties, and No. 7112 was withdrawn in 1949.

Thursday 22 August 1946. *Above*: Seen here in Lowestoft shed yard is ex-GER Class C32 (LNER Class F3) 2-4-2 tank No. 8097. Again designed by James Holden for suburban passenger traffic, in later life most would be relegated to empty coach workings or country branch line work. One of fifty examples constructed at Stratford Works, No. 8097, built in 1893, would be withdrawn during August 1947. *Opposite*: Originally constructed at Stratford Works in 1908 as a Class D56 locomotive for the Great Eastern Railway, 'Claud Hamilton' No. 2568 (seen here in Lowestoft shed yard) would be rebuilt during 1933 utilising a superheating boiler and be classified by the LNER as Class D16. As the principal express passenger locomotives of the GER prior to the introduction of their 4-6-0 wheel arrangement locomotives, they would be seen on all the main routes out of London Liverpool Street station. After the grouping they could be found on Cambridge expresses running out of Kings Cross station and were utilised on secondary routes in later years. Of the 121 examples constructed, all except four had been withdrawn by the end of 1959. No. 2568 would become 62568 with British Railways and would be withdrawn during 1958.

The three illustrations here show the very pleasing lines of the ex-GER Class T26 (LNER Class E4) 2-4-0s, designed by James Holden as mixed traffic locomotives. Introduced during 1891, a total of 100 examples were constructed, all coming from Stratford Works, with the last appearing in 1902. *Left, top:* **Friday 23 August 1946**. Seen here in Cambridge shed yard is No 7492: she would be renumbered 2786 a few months later and finally become No. 62786 with British Railways. Constructed during 1895, she would finally be withdrawn in 1956. *Left, bottom:* **Tuesday 1 October 1946**. Seen in Norwich shed yard is sister locomotive No. 2787. Also built in 1895, she would become No. 62787 and would be withdrawn during 1956. *Opposite:* **Tuesday 1 October 1946**. No. 2792 is also seen in Norwich shed yard, sporting a stovepipe chimney. An example of the 1902 build, she would be renumbered 62792 and would be withdrawn in 1956.

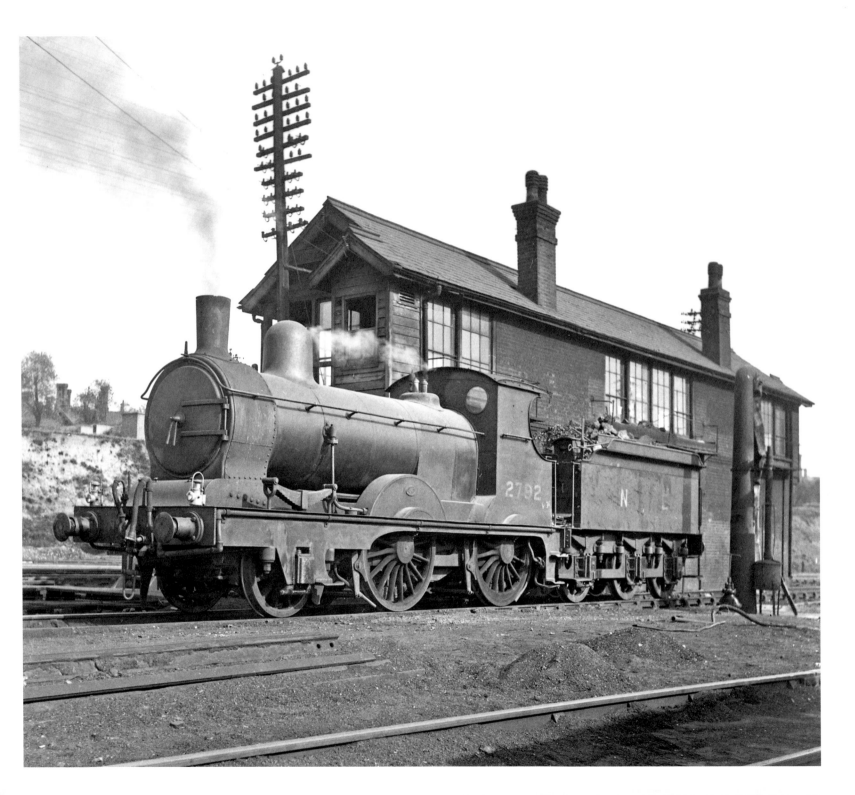

Tuesday 1 October 1946. *Above:* Ex-GER Class R24 (LNER Class J69) 0-6-0 tank No. 8570 is seen here in Norwich shed yard wearing her newly allocated number. Constructed at Stratford Works during 1896, she was formerly numbered 7394, before becoming No. 68570 with British Railways. She would be withdrawn in 1961, having given sixty-five years of service. *Opposite, top:* Designed by Henry Ivatt for the GNR and introduced during 1898, his Class D1 (LNER Class D2) 4-4-0s were primarily designed for utilisation on secondary passenger work, particularly around Nottinghamshire and Lincolnshire. No. 4329 is seen here at Melton Constable shed, the centre of the M&GNJR territory. She would be renumbered 2157 during the following month and would finally be withdrawn from service in 1948. *Opposite, bottom:* This James Holden design of a powerful goods locomotive appeared during 1900, with construction continuing until 1911 when the final two examples entered service. Ex-GER Class G58 (LNER Class J17) 0-6-0 No. 5586 was the product of Stratford Works during 1910, and is seen here in Melton Constable yard. Rebuilt with a superheating boiler during 1930, she would be renumbered 65586 before being withdrawn in 1962.

Tuesday 1 October 1946. This diminutive tank locomotive is one of only nine examples constructed by the M&GNJR at their Melton Constable Works between 1897 and 1905. Designed by their engineer William Marriott, examples of the class were allocated to Yarmouth Beach, Norwich City, South Lynn, and Melton Constable for shunting and station pilot duties. Classified J93 by the LNER, No. 016 is seen here in Melton Constable yard: she was the last example of the class to be constructed, during 1905, and the last example to be withdrawn in 1949.

Wednesday 2 October 1946. Seen here at Wisbech shed yard are two classes of ex-GER 'Tram Locomotive' that were designed specifically to operate on the Wisbech and Upwell Tramway and the Yarmouth Union Tramway, both of which involved some street workings. *Top*: Ex-GER Class G15 (LNER Class Y6) 0-4-0 No. 8083 was designed by Thomas Worsdell and constructed at Stratford Works during 1897. Previously numbered 7134 by the LNER, this locomotive spent some wartime years working for the armed forces in UK depots, before being numbered 68083 and withdrawn in 1952. *Bottom*: Ex-GER Class C53 (LNER Class J70) 0-6-0 No. 8223 was of a James Holden design and constructed during 1914 at Stratford Works. She was later numbered 68223, before being withdrawn in 1955. Several examples of this class were also allocated at Ipswich shed to work in the docks there.

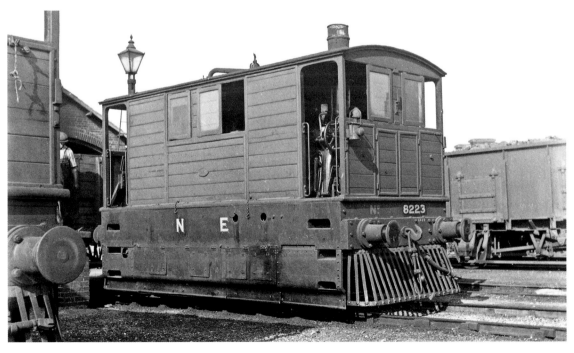

Monday 9 June 1947. Edward Thompson's first design for the LNER was a 4-6-0 mixed traffic locomotive that entered service during 1942; this was the Class B1, of which 410 examples were constructed, with the last appearing during 1950. Over a period of several years, a total of 290 were supplied by the NBL, with the Vulcan Foundry building fifty examples and the remainder coming from both Darlington and Gorton Works. Seen here at the head of the 2.20 p.m. Cleethorpes to Retford service at Gainsborough Central station is No. 1152: delivered from the Vulcan Foundry in the month prior to this photograph, she would be withdrawn from service only seventeen years later in 1964.

Sunday 21 March 1948. *Top*: Seen here at Stratford shed wearing her new owners' identity, is another example of ex-LNER Class B1 4-6-0 No. 61049 in ex-works condition. Constructed by the NBL in 1946, she would be withdrawn during 1965. *Bottom*: Sitting in the yard at Stratford Works minus connecting rods is WD 2-8-0 No. 78675, newly returned from Europe after wartime service. Constructed by the Vulcan Foundry during 1944, she would see service on the Detmold Military Railway in Germany and be named *Sapper* – the blank name board can be seen above the running plate. After refurbishment, she would be purchased by British Railways and numbered 90644, giving a further twenty years of service before being withdrawn during 1967.

Sunday 21 March 1948. *Above*: Designed by Nigel Gresley as a class of express goods locomotives, his highly successful three-cylinder Class H4 2-6-0 for the GNR first appeared during 1920. Classified K3 by the LNER, they were allocated widely throughout that company's territory and were equally at ease handling passenger traffic. No. 1981, a product of Darlington Works in 1936, as seen here at Stratford shed. After becoming 61981 with British Railways, she would be withdrawn in 1962. *Opposite, top*: Standing in Stratford shed yard in ex-works condition and bearing her new owners' identity and number is ex-GER Class Y14 (LNER Class J15) E5452. Constructed at the same works in 1906, she would later become number 65452 before being withdrawn during 1959. *Opposite, bottom*: Also seen in ex-works condition at Stratford shed is ex-GER Class S56 (LNER Class J69) 0-6-0 tank No. E8619, which was constructed at Stratford Works during 1904. Resplendent in LNER green livery, she was working as pilot at Liverpool Street station and would remain so until withdrawal in 1961.

Saturday 24 April 1948. *Above*: At Melton Mowbray Midland station, ex-MR Class 2 (LMS Class 2P) 4-4-0 No. 395 waits to depart with a passenger train. Constructed at Derby Works during 1891, she would later be rebuilt, before finally being withdrawn in 1954. *Opposite, top*: At Melton Mowbray Joint station, ex-LMS Class 3P 2-6-2 tank No. 52 is seen working a train to Market Harborough and Northampton. Designed by Henry Fowler and introduced during 1930, this class of seventy parallel-boilered locomotives were all constructed at Derby Works, with No. 52 appearing in 1932. She would be withdrawn from service during 1959. *Opposite, bottom*: Ex-LMS Class 8F 2-8-0 No. 8624, bearing a 1A Willesden shed code, is drifting through Melton Mowbray Joint station at the head of a train of mineral wagons. Constructed as part of a Railway Executive order at the Southern Railway Ashford Works during 1943, she would go on to become 48624 with British Railways before being withdrawn in 1965. She spent many years at Woodham's yard at Barry, but was purchased for preservation and returned to steam in 2009. She is currently based at the Great Central Railway at Loughborough.

Saturday 11 September 1948. Recognised as probably the most reliable of the pre-grouping heavy goods locomotive classes to be designed by a constituent company of the LNER, the John Robinson Class 8K 2-8-0 (LNER Class O4) for the GCR played a major role in both the First and Second World Wars, with large numbers of the class being shipped abroad to assist the armed forces. With over 400 examples constructed over a period of nine years, the LNER purchased 273 examples from the War Department during the 1920s. *Above*: Seen here in Annesley shed yard, No. 3794 was a product of the NBL during 1918 for the Railway Operating Division (ROD), and would be numbered 1898 by them. Acquired by the LNER during 1924, she would finally be numbered 63794 by British Railways and then be withdrawn in 1962. *Opposite, top*: Bearing her new owners' identity, No. 63748 is seen here in Annesley shed yard. Constructed by the NBL for the ROD (Railway Operating Division) during 1917, she would also be acquired by the LNER during 1924 and be destined for withdrawal in 1962. *Opposite, bottom*: This example of the class, again seen in Annesley shed yard, is No. 3589. From a batch constructed by the NBL during 1912, she would be rebuilt as a Class O1 during 1949 and numbered 63589 by British Railways, before being withdrawn in 1965.

Saturday 11 September 1948. *Opposite, top:* Another ex-GCR Class 8K (LNER Class O4) 2-8-0 seen here in Annesley shed is No. 63605. This example was the product of Gorton Works during 1913 and would be withdrawn in 1962. *Opposite, bottom:* Seen outside her normal territory, ex-NER Class T2 (LNER Class Q6) 0-8-0 No. 3382 is at Annesley shed. Built at Darlington Works during 1917, she would be renumbered 63382 and withdrawn in 1964. *Above:* Preparing to leave Annesley shed is ex-GCR Class 8K (LNER Class O4) 2-8-0 No. 63759. Another member of the class constructed by the NBL for the ROD during 1918, she would be numbered 1848 by them, before being purchased by the LNER in 1924 and being withdrawn during 1962.

Friday 12 May 1950. At Nottingham Midland station, ex-MR Class 2 (LMS Class 3F) 0-6-0 No. 43634 is waiting to depart with the 7.40 p.m. working to Worksop. From a design by Samuel Johnson, this example came from the works of Dübs & Co. in Glasgow during 1900. She would be rebuilt in the form seen here with a Belpaire firebox during the Henry Fowler period, and she would give sixty years' service before being withdrawn in 1960.

Saturday 20 May 1950. Still bearing her LMS identity on the tender, ex-MR Class 2 (LMS Class 2P) 4-4-0 No. 40528 is preparing to depart from Leicester London Road station with the 1.10 p.m. train to Nuneaton Trent Valley station. She was constructed at Derby Works during 1899 and would be withdrawn in 1953.

Saturday 20 May 1950. This wonderfully atmospheric photograph taken within the confines of Leicester London Road station shows Class 4MT 2-6-0 No. 43045 pausing with the 8.15 a.m. Lowestoft Central to Birmingham New Street working. Designed by Henry George Ivatt for the LMS as a mixed-traffic locomotive, the class was introduced during 1947, with only the first three examples appearing before nationalisation. No. 43045 was a product of Horwich Works during 1949: she would only give seventeen years' service before being withdrawn in 1966.

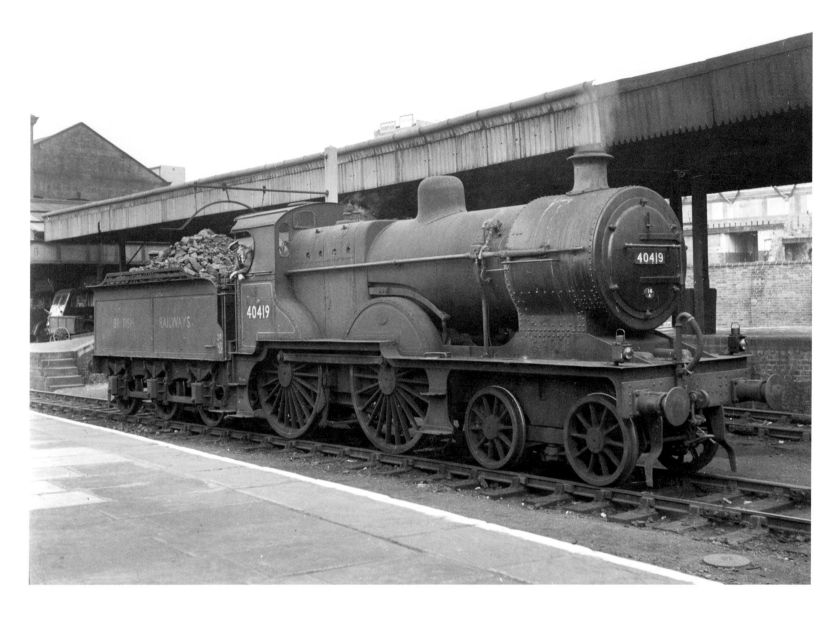

Saturday 5 August 1950. Standing in Nottingham Midland station awaiting its next duty is ex-MR Class 2 (LMS Class 2P) 4-4-0 No. 40419. Constructed by Sharp Stewart & Co. during 1892, she would be withdrawn in 1955.

Saturday 2 September 1950. At Grantham station, ex-LNER Class V2 2-6-2 No. 60902 is seen at the head of the 11.00 a.m. Filey to London Kings Cross working. Another successful design from Nigel Gresley, the class was introduced in 1936, with No. 60902 coming from Darlington Works during 1940. Originally numbered 4873 and then 902 with the LNER, she would be withdrawn during 1963.

Saturday 2 September 1950. Ex-LNER Class A4 4-6-2 No. 60004 *William Whitelaw* is seen here at speed entering Grantham station with the 'up' 'Capitals Limited'. Constructed at Doncaster Works during 1937, where she was originally numbered 4462 and named *Great Snipe*, she would be renamed after the first chairman of the LNER in 1941. She is seen here in the short-lived British Railways blue livery while she was allocated to Haymarket shed in Edinburgh. Finally allocated to Ferryhill shed in Aberdeen, she would be withdrawn in 1966. This non-stop summer-only London to Edinburgh service utilised Class A4 locomotives fitted with corridor tenders and commenced during 1949; in 1953, the name was changed to 'The Elizabethan' to mark the coronation of Elizabeth II. The service ceased during 1962.

Saturday 2 September 1950. *Opposite*: Designed by John Robinson for the GCR as a replacement for the earlier tank locomotives operating the suburban services out of Marylebone station, the impressive-looking Class 9N 4-6-2 tanks were introduced during 1911, with building continuing in batches until 1926. Classified A5 by the LNER, they became widely allocated throughout their territory, operating as far north as Gateshead. Seen here at Grantham station, No. 69813 has just arrived with the 2.10 p.m. working from Lincoln. Constructed at Gorton Works during 1912, she would be withdrawn in 1960. *Right, top*: Speeding through Grantham station at the head of the 12.05 p.m. Newcastle to London Kings Cross express is the yet-to-be-named Class A1 4-6-2 No. 60144. Barely a year into her service life, having left Darlington Works early in 1949, she would be named *Kings Courier* in January 1951. Designed by Arthur Peppercorn, none of the forty-nine examples built would see much more than fifteen years' service, with No. 60144 being withdrawn in 1963. *Right, bottom*: Ex-WD Class 8F 2-8-0 No. 90648 is seen plodding through Grantham station with an 'up' train of mineral wagons. Built by the Vulcan Foundry during 1944, she would be numbered 78684 by the War Department and come into LNER ownership in 1947, before passing to British Railways on nationalisation. She would be withdrawn during 1962.

Opposite: **Saturday 2 September 1950**. Designed by Stephen Holden, the impressive-looking ex-GER Class S69 (LNER Class B12) 4-6-0s provided the increased power to handle the heavier express passenger services out of Liverpool Street station. No. 61538 is seen here at Grantham station; constructed at Stratford Works during 1915, she would be rebuilt in 1937 with a larger firebox and boiler and classified B12/3, before being withdrawn in 1957. *Above:* **Saturday 2 September 1950**. Having stopped 'out of course' at Grantham station, the 'up' 'Flying Scotsman' prepares to restart. Ex-LNER Class A4 4-6-2 No. 60030 *Golden Fleece* was allocated to Kings Cross shed during this time – constructed at Doncaster Works during 1937, she was only ever allocated to two sheds during her working life: Kings Cross and Grantham. Seen here in the short-lived blue livery applied by British Railways, she would be withdrawn in 1962.

Saturday 16 September 1950. Bearing a 15D Bedford shed code, ex-LMS Class 4P 'Compound' 4-4-0 No. 41070 is waiting her next duty at Bedford shed. A 1924 Derby Works-built example of this class, she would be withdrawn during 1955.

Saturday 16 September 1950. Seen arriving at Bedford Midland Road station at the head of the 12.15 p.m. service from Northampton is ex-MR Class '2611' (LMS Class 1P) 0-4-4 tank No. 58089, still bearing her former owners' identity on the tank side. Designed by Samuel Johnson and formerly numbered 1426 by the LMS, she was a product of Dübs & Co. during 1900 that would be withdrawn by British Railways in 1954.

Saturday 16 September 1950. Ex-LMS Class 4P 'Compound' 4-4-0 No. 41091 is waiting to depart from Bedford Midland Road station with the 1.05 p.m. service to London St Pancras. Constructed at Derby Works during 1925, these LMS versions of the Midland Railway Class 1000 'Compounds' utilised 6ft 9in driving wheels instead of the original's 7' dimension. Bearing a 15D Bedford shed code, the example seen here would be withdrawn during 1955.

Saturday 16 September 1950. Waiting to depart from Bedford Midland Road station at the head of the 1.35 p.m. to London St Pancras is ex-MR Class 1000 'Compound' 4-4-0 No. 41020. An example of the class constructed during the Richard Deeley period at Derby Works, she entered service during 1906 and was rebuilt with a superheating boiler during 1922. Seen here bearing a 14B Kentish Town shed code, she would be withdrawn during 1951.

Saturday 3 March 1951. Withdrawn from service during the month prior to this photograph, ex-GER Class Y14 (LNER Class J15) 0-6-0 No. 5350 awaits her fate at Stratford shed. Constructed at Stratford Works during 1886, she had seen sixty-five years of service.

Saturday 3 March 1951. In Stratford shed yard, ex-GER Class D56 (LNER Class D16) 4-4-0 No. 62598 in a grimy condition. Constructed at Stratford Works during 1910, she would be rebuilt in 1942 as a Class D16 locomotive, before being withdrawn in 1952.

Saturday 3 March 1951. Edward Thompson's only tank locomotive design for the LNER was the Class L1 2-6-4 tank, with the first example appearing during 1945. After extensive testing, the first of the production locomotives entered service after nationalisation in 1948. Not a complete success due to mechanical failures, some examples only served for eleven years before being withdrawn. Constructed by the NBL during 1948, No. 67735 is seen here at Stratford shed; she would be withdrawn in 1962.

Saturday 3 March 1951. Sitting in Stratford shed yard is ex-LNER Class B1 4-6-0 No. 61233. A product of the NBL during 1947, she would be transferred during her 1963 withdrawal to British Railways service stock and be nominally numbered 21 within department stock. Utilised as a stationary boiler, she would finally be withdrawn from service in 1966.

Saturday 18 August 1951. At the head of an 'up' express and seen passing Retford North signal box is ex-LNER Class A3 4-6-2 No. 60102 *Sir Frederick Banbury*. Bearing a 38C Leicester shed code, she was something of a wanderer throughout her working life, having spent time allocated to Doncaster, Neasden, Kings Cross and Grantham sheds in addition to Leicester. Constructed at Doncaster Works during 1922 as a Class A1 for the GNR, she would be rebuilt as a Class A3 locomotive in 1942 and be withdrawn during 1961. She carries the name of the last chairman of the Great Northern Railway. In the background is ex-LNER Class J39 0-6-0 No. 64885; built at Darlington Works during 1935, she would also be withdrawn in 1961.

Left, top: **Saturday 18 August 1951**. Seen here at speed passing Dukeries Junction with the 8 a.m. South Shields to London Kings Cross working is the Arthur Peppercorn-designed Class A1 4-6-2 No. 60135 *Madge Wildfire*. Constructed at Darlington Works during 1948, she would spend the bulk of her working life allocated to Gateshead shed and would be withdrawn after only fourteen years of service in 1962. She bore the name of a character that appears in the novel *The Heart of Midlothian* by Sir Walter Scott. *Left, bottom*: **Monday 20 August 1951**. Shunting in Warsop Colliery sidings is ex-LNER Class Q1 0-8-0 tank No. 69928. Originally constructed as a John Robinson design of Class 8A 0-8-0 tender locomotive for the GCR, she was a product of Gorton Works during 1909 and was destined to be rebuilt by Edward Thompson as a tank locomotive in 1943, before being withdrawn during 1959. *Opposite*: **Thursday 23 August 1951**. In ex-works condition, ex-GNR Class J22 (LNER Class J6) 0-6-0 No. 64179 is seen about to enter Dukeries Junction with an 'up' mixed goods train. Designed by Henry Ivatt utilising a superheated boiler and introduced in 1911, the class continued construction with minor alterations under Nigel Gresley up to 1922, when a total of 110 examples had entered service. Bearing a 36A Doncaster shed code, No. 64179 was an early member of the class from 1911 that would be withdrawn during 1960.

Thursday 23 August 1951. This spread shows two examples of Nigel Gresley's masterpiece Class A4 Pacific design, both at Dukeries Junction. *Opposite*: At the head of the 'up' 'Capitals Limited' is No. 60009 *Union of South Africa*. Constructed during 1937 at Doncaster Works, she was allocated new to Haymarket shed in Edinburgh until 1962, when she was transferred to Ferryhill in Aberdeen, where she would be withdrawn in 1966. Purchased privately, she has since been seen working many main-line specials throughout the UK. *Above*: No. 60030 *Golden Fleece* is seen working the 11.55 a.m. Newcastle to London Kings Cross service.

Saturday 5 January 1952. *Opposite*: At Bedford shed ex-MR Class 1000 (LMS Class 4P) 'Compound' 4-4-0 No. 41038 is looking in good clean condition. Another example of the Richard Deeley modifications of Samuel Johnson's original work, she was constructed at Derby Works during 1908 and would be rebuilt with a superheating boiler in 1922, and would not be withdrawn until 1952. *Right, top*: Seen here at Wellingborough shed, bearing a 16C Kirkby-in-Ashfield shed code, is an early example of William Stanier's highly successful LMS Class 8F 2-8-0. No. 48006 was constructed as part of the first batch of this class during 1935 at Crewe Works and would be withdrawn after thirty years' service in 1965. *Right, bottom*: Beyer Peacock & Co. constructed thirty-three Beyer Garratt 2-6-0+0-6-2 Class locomotives for the LMS during 1927 and 1930, primarily to haul the heavy coal trains from the Nottinghamshire collieries to Brent in London with many of the class being based at Toton shed. Others of the class were based at Wellingborough, and seen here at that shed is No. 47974, which was from the 1930 build. Originally running with straight-sided coal bunkers, all except two were rebuilt with rotary bunkers as seen here. No. 47974 would be withdrawn during 1956.

Saturday 24 May 1952. *Opposite*: Bearing a 40B Immingham shed code, Class B1 4-6-0 No. 61379 *Mayflower* pauses in Spalding station with a 'down' stopper. Constructed by the NBL during 1951, she was given her name soon after entering service, but would be one of the early class withdrawals in 1962, having given only eleven years of service. *Right, top*: Ex-GER Class S46 (LNER Class D14) 4-4-0 No. 62534 is seen here at Kings Lynn station. Constructed at Stratford Works during 1903 utilising a saturated steam boiler, she would be rebuilt during 1926 with a superheating boiler and classified D15 by the LNER, before being reclassified D16 by them during 1935. She would be withdrawn from service in 1958. *Right, bottom*: Another member of the class is seen here at Kings Lynn shed, No. 62514 was a 1901 product of Stratford Works that would be rebuilt with a superheating boiler in 1916. Classified D15 by the LNER she would be reclassified D16 by them during 1943 and be withdrawn in 1957.

Saturday 24 May 1952. Ex-GER Class T26 (LNER Class E4) 2-4-0 No. 62787 is seen here at Kings Lynn station; she would be withdrawn during 1956 after sixty years of service.

Saturday 24 May 1952. The very well-balanced lines of the GER 'Claud Hamilton' class are seen here with No. 62577 standing in Wells-on-Sea station yard being prepared to work the 1.35 p.m. departure to Heacham. Constructed at Stratford Works during 1909 as a Class D56 for the GER, she would be rebuilt with a superheating boiler in 1922 and reclassified D16 by the LNER in 1929. She would be withdrawn during 1956.

Saturday 24 May 1952. Seen here approaching Kings Lynn station with an auto train working from South Lynn is ex-GNR Class C2 (LNER Class C12) 4-4-2 tank No. 67386. Designed by Henry Ivatt and constructed at Doncaster Works during 1903, she would be specifically fitted during 1949 for 'push-pull' operation on this branch and be withdrawn in 1958.

Saturday 21 June 1952. Seen here in Grantham station is ex-LNER Class V2 2-6-2 No. 60956 which was constructed at Darlington Works during 1942. The class was designed with three cylinders in one monobloc casting, but these became susceptible to cracking; consequently, of the 184 examples constructed, a total of seventy-one were rebuilt over a period of years using three separate cylinder castings. This necessitated the use of outside exhaust steam pipes, which easily identified these rebuilt locomotives. No. 60956 would be rebuilt with separate cylinders in 1959 and withdrawn during 1962.

Saturday 28 June 1952. This day saw the running of the Stephenson Locomotive Society's Derbyshire Area Railtour, starting at Derby Midland station and taking in Melbourne, Worthington and Ashby-de-la-Zouch before returning to Derby. Motive power was the Samuel Johnson-designed ex-MR Class '2611' (LMS Class 1P) 0-4-4 tank No. 58087, which is seen here at Ashby-de-la-Zouch. Bearing a 17B Burton shed code, she was constructed by Dübs & Co. during 1900 and would be finally withdrawn in 1960.

Saturday 9 May 1953. At Worksop station, ex-MR Class 2 (LMS Class 2P) 4-4-0 No. 40487 is waiting to depart with a passenger train. Originally constructed at Derby Works during 1898, she would give sixty-three years of service before being withdrawn in 1961.

Saturday 9 May 1953. *Opposite, top*: Arriving at Retford station at the head of the 12.25 p.m. Leeds to London Kings Cross train is ex-LNER Class A3 4-6-2 No. 60110 *Robert the Devil*. Constructed at Doncaster Works during 1923 as a Class A1 locomotive, she would be rebuilt as a Class A3 in 1942 and withdrawn during 1963. She carries the name of the 1880 winner of the St Leger horse race. *Opposite, bottom*: Standing in Retford Great Central shed yard is ex-GNR Class J4 (LNER Class J3) 0-6-0 No. 64141. Based on an original design by Patrick Stirling, Henry Ivatt continued the construction of this 'Standard Goods' class of locomotive with various modifications. No. 64141 was constructed in 1900 at Doncaster Works and would become No. 3387 and later 4141 with the LNER. She would be withdrawn during 1953. *Above*: **Sunday 4 April 1954**. Seen here in Kings Cross shed yard in a filthy condition is Class L1 2-6-4 tank No. 67720. Built at Darlington Works during 1948, she would be withdrawn after only fourteen years' service in 1962.

This spread shows three examples of the ex-GNR Class C2 (LNER Class C12) 4-4-2 tank locomotive operating rural passenger services. *Left, top*: **Monday 13 September 1954**. In England's smallest county, Rutland, the ex-LNWR branch from Seaton to Uppingham still appeared in the London Midland Region timetable, but utilised ex-LNER locomotive stock. No. 67368 is waiting to depart from Uppingham station with the 12.24 p.m. train to the junction at Seaton. Constructed at Doncaster Works during 1899, she would be withdrawn in 1955. *Left, bottom*: **Tuesday 14 September 1954**. No. 67384 is seen arriving at Willoughby station with the 9.49 a.m. train from Louth via Mablethorpe: the locomotive would run round its train and return to Louth as the 11.04 a.m. departure. Built at Doncaster Works in 1903, this locomotive would be withdrawn during 1956. *Opposite*: **Tuesday 14 September 1954**. At Mablethorpe station, a very clean No. 67398 is preparing to depart with the 1.46 p.m. Louth to Sutton-on-Sea working. Constructed at Doncaster Works during 1907, she would be one of the last members of the class to be withdrawn towards the end of 1958.

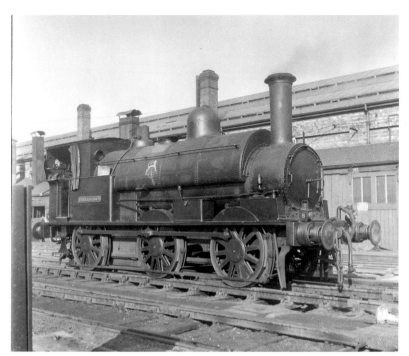

Saturday 19 March 1955. A visit to Wolverton Carriage Works in Buckinghamshire gave the photographer the opportunity to photograph the four ex-LNWR 0-6-0 'Special Tanks' in steam. Designed by John Ramsbottom and introduced during 1870 (with construction continuing until 1880), a total of 260 entered service, all having been constructed at Crewe Works with open cabs. They comprised the following: *Above left*: No. CD8 bearing the name *Earlstown* was built during 1879 and originally numbered 2359 by the LNWR. Transferred to Earlstown Wagon Works near Warrington during 1881, she would be transferred to Wolverton Carriage Works in 1938 to be numbered CD8 and would be withdrawn during 1957, having given seventy-eight years' service. *Above right*: No. CD6 is carrying the description *CARRE DEPT WOLN* and is also fitted with a Westinghouse pump. Constructed during 1875, she was originally numbered 186 by the LNWR and transferred to Wolverton Carriage Works in 1901. She gave eighty-four years' service, being withdrawn in 1959. *Left*: No. CD7 is bearing a plate with the description *CARR DEPT WOL No. 7*. She was constructed during 1878 and numbered 2329 by the LNW, but went on to bear a series of numbers, eventually becoming CD7 during 1911 on transfer to Wolverton Carriage Works. CD7 was the last of the class to be withdrawn in 1959, after eighty-one years' service. *Opposite*: No. CD3 bears the description *CARR DEPT WOL*. Constructed during 1880 and numbered 317 by the LNWR, she was transferred to Wolverton Carriage Works in 1897 and numbered CD3. She would give seventy-nine years of service before being withdrawn during 1959.

Saturday 24 September 1955. This British Railways Standard Class 2 design was directly derived from the Henry George Ivatt Class 2MT 2-6-2 tanks for the LMS. Only thirty examples were constructed, with the first twenty appearing from Crewe Works during 1953 and the final ten from Darlington Works in 1957. Seen here at Kegworth station is No. 84006, bearing a 17B Burton shed code, which has arrived with the RCTS East Midlands Branch Kegworth Railtour. A product of Crewe Works in 1953, she would be withdrawn during 1965.

Saturday 24 September 1955. Ex-LMS Class 4P 'Compound' 4-4-0 No. 41097 is seen entering Kegworth station with the 5.08 p.m. Nottingham to Leicester working. Bearing a 15C Leicester shed code, she was constructed at Derby Works during 1925 and withdrawn in 1956.

Saturday 29 October 1955. The London Tilbury and Southend Railway was initially opened to Tilbury in 1854, with Southend being reached in 1856 and Shoeburyness in 1884. Purchased by the Midland Railway during 1912, the LT&SR utilised a series of 4-4-2 tanks, with the most noteworthy being their Class 79 designed by Thomas Whitelegg and introduced during 1909. Further batches were constructed after the grouping, and seen here at Southend Central station is Class 79 (LMS Class 3P) No. 41939. Constructed as part of a batch of five examples by Nasmyth Wilson & Co. during 1925, she would initially be numbered 2121 by the LMS and would be withdrawn in 1959.

Saturday 29 October 1955. In response to the need for a modern locomotive to operate the intensive LT&SR services, the LMS introduced a three cylinder 2-6-4 tank class and constructed thirty-seven examples at Derby works during 1934. Seen here at Shoeburyness station, having arrived with the 11.35 a.m. from London Fenchurch Street, is the William Stanier-designed Class 4P No. 42512; she would be the first of the class to be withdrawn during 1960.

Saturday 3 March 1956. Photographed on a wet and overcast day within the limiting confines of Moorgate station, ex-GNR Class N2 (LNER Class N2) 0-6-2 tank No. 69537 is departing with the 11.43 a.m. service to New Barnet. Constructed by the NBL during 1921, she would be withdrawn from service in 1959. This 11-mile journey was timetabled to take 38 minutes, with the first 2 miles to Kings Cross station including a tortuous curved 1 in 43 gradient through tunnels leading to platform sixteen at Kings Cross. Having departed from Kings Cross and negotiated the Gas Works tunnel, the remainder of the journey was at least in the open air.

Thursday 13 September 1956. This spread shows the ex-Metropolitan Railway branch at Chesham. *Opposite*: ex-GCR Class 9K (LNER Class C13) 4-4-2 tank No. 67420 takes water before departing with the 2.08 p.m. working to Chalfont and Latimer. *Right*: The same locomotive is seen departing from Chesham with the 2.35 p.m. departure to the junction at Chalfont and Latimer. Designed by John Robinson and introduced during 1903, a total of forty examples were constructed by both Gorton Works and the Vulcan Foundry and utilised to work the suburban traffic from Marylebone; constructed at Gorton Works during 1904, 67420 would be withdrawn in 1958. Three members of the class based at Neasden were fitted with push-pull equipment and allocated to this branch work from 1941, but in 1958 they were replaced by ex-LMS Class 2 2-6-2 tanks.

Saturday 27 April 1957. The Stephenson Locomotive Society Nottinghamshire Coalfield Tour has reached Bestwood Park with BR Standard Class 2MT 2-6-2 tank No. 84006 in charge, seen here taking water. Standing adjacent in the sidings is ex-LMS Class 8F 2-8-0 No. 48748, which was constructed at the LNER Darlington Works during 1946 and entered service with the LNER number of 3143, which then changed to 3543. She would become LMS No. 8748 before nationalisation and would be withdrawn from service in 1966.

Saturday 10 August 1957. Waiting to depart from Nottingham Victoria station at the head of the 1.35 p.m. train to Ollerton is ex-GCR Class 9N (LNER Class A5) 4-6-2 tank No. 69816. Constructed at Gorton Works during 1917, she would be withdrawn in 1959.

Thursday 1 May 1958. In ex-works condition, ex-LNER Class V2 2-6-2 No. 60821 is seen at Grantham station and bearing a 35B Grantham shed code. She was constructed at Darlington Works during 1937 and rebuilt with separate cylinders in February 1958 (as is seen by the use of outside exhaust steam pipes), before being withdrawn in 1962.

Opposite, top: **Saturday 26 July 1958**. At the head of a 'down' train of mineral wagons, ex-LMS Class 8F 2-8-0 No. 48082 is passing through Market Harborough station – note the amount of wagon traffic in the busy goods yard. Constructed by the Vulcan Foundry during 1937, 48082 would be withdrawn in 1967. *Opposite, bottom:* **Saturday 2 August 1958**. Parked in Retford shed yard is ex-GCR Class 8K (LNER Class O4) 2-8-0 No. 63818. Originally constructed by the NBL during 1918 for the ROD and numbered 1936 by them, she would be purchased by the LNER in 1924 and numbered 6264 and later 3818 by that company. She was selected as one of the O4 class to be rebuilt by Edward Thompson in 1947 as an O4/8, with a larger boiler and firebox, and she would be withdrawn from service during 1966. Note that she is still bearing the diamond-shaped NBL builders' works plate. *Above:* **Saturday 2 August 1958**. Seen approaching Retford at the head of the 'down' 'Queen of Scots' Pullman, Class A1 4-6-2 No. 60134 *Foxhunter* has a relatively easy load of eight coaches. She was constructed at Darlington Works during 1950 and carried the name of the winner of the 1932 Doncaster Cup horse race. Allocated to Copley Hill for the bulk of her working life, she would be withdrawn in 1965. The 'Queen of Scots' Pullman service commenced during 1928 and, by 1958, took just over nine hours to complete the journey from London Kings Cross to Leeds, Newcastle, Edinburgh and Glasgow. The service ceased during 1964.

Saturday 28 February 1959. This was the last day of passenger services over the greater part of the old Midland and Great Northern Joint Railway (M&GNJR) routes that wandered through East Anglia. The company was formed by the Midland Railway and the Great Northern Railway, who had acquired a number of smaller companies that gave them access to the East Anglian ports from the East Midlands. Traffic consisted mainly of coal heading east and agricultural products and fish heading west, with the summer holiday traffic seeing many special trains running. At its centre of operations were the locomotive and engineering workshops at Melton Constable, which would be closed after the LNER took control during 1936. *Left, top*: Two young enthusiasts witness Class 4MT 2-6-0 No. 43088 entering Peterborough North station with the 6.59 a.m. working from Yarmouth Beach. Carrying a 34E New England shed code, she was constructed at Darlington Works during 1950 and would be withdrawn in 1967. *Left, bottom*: Class 4MT 2-6-0 No. 43150 has arrived at Norwich City station in a filthy condition at the head of the 1.43 p.m. train from Melton Constable. Bearing a 32G Melton Constable shed code, she was a product of Doncaster Works in 1951 that would give only fourteen years of service before being withdrawn during 1965. *Opposite*: Bearing a 31D South Lynn shed code and in a much cleaner condition, Class 4MT 2-6-0 No. 43111 is seen at Sutton Bridge station with the 11.11 a.m. Peterborough North to Yarmouth Beach. Another example from Doncaster Works that entered service in 1951, she would also be withdrawn during 1965.

Saturday 18 April 1959. Nigel Gresley designed the three-cylinder Class B17 4-6-0s specifically for express passenger traffic on the Great Eastern section of the LNER, and they were introduced during 1928. A total of seventy-three entered service, the last appearing during 1937, and ten examples were rebuilt by Edward Thompson with two cylinders and classified B2 during his period as CME. Standing in the yard at Stratford shed is No. 61618 *Wynyard Park*, which was a Darlington Works-constructed example from 1930 that would be withdrawn in 1960.

Saturday 18 April 1959. In Stratford shed yard Class L1 2-6-4 tank No. 67739 is in good clean condition. Constructed by the NBL during 1948, she would be withdrawn in 1961 after only thirteen years of service.

Saturday 18 April 1959. Ex-GER Class L77 (LNER Class N7) 0-6-2 tank No. 69615 is in Stratford shed yard in ex-works condition. Designed by Alfred Hill to supply a tank locomotive suitable for handling the suburban traffic out of Liverpool Street station, 134 examples were constructed over a period of thirteen years from 1915 until 1928. In addition to Gorton, Stratford and Doncaster Works, both Robert Stephenson & Co. and William Beardmore & Co. supplied examples; No. 69615 was a product of Stratford Works in 1924 that would be withdrawn during 1960.

Saturday 18 April 1959. In Stratford shed yard, ex-GER Class Y14 (LNER Class J15) 0-6-0 No. 65361 is in filthy condition. Constructed at Stratford Works during 1889, she would become one of the longest-serving members of the class, giving seventy-three years before her withdrawal in 1962.

Sunday 10 April 1960. *Above*: The locomotive pictured here had an interesting history, originally constructed as a GCR Class 8K 2-8-0 by the NBL in 1919 for the ROD who would number her 2144. She was acquired by the LNER during 1927 and re-numbered 6639 and classified O4 by that company. When Edward Thompson took over from Nigel Gresley in 1941, he planned to modernise members of class O4, utilising larger boilers and fireboxes and new cylinders with Walschaerts piston valve gear. A total of fifty-eight were rebuilt and classified O1 by the LNER with No. 63890, seen here at March shed, coming out of Gorton Works during 1946. She would be withdrawn in 1963. *Opposite*: A comparison is seen here at New England shed of two major classes of heavy goods locomotive, both designed by Robert Riddles and utilised by British Railways in large numbers. *Top*: BR Standard Class 9F 2-10-0 No. 92178 was constructed at Swindon Works during 1957, but she would see only eight years of service before being withdrawn in 1965. *Bottom*: Ex-WD Class 8F 2-8-0 No. 90246 was constructed for the War Department by the NBL in 1943 and numbered 77338. Shipped to Europe after D-Day, she worked with the Nederlandse Spoorwegen (NS) in Holland during 1945 and returned to the UK in 1947, before also being withdrawn during 1965.

Sunday 10 April 1960. *Above*: Parked in the yard at New England shed is an example of the Edward Thompson 'Standard' design of Pacific locomotive for the LNER. Introduced during 1946; only fifteen examples were constructed at Doncaster Works, as Thompson retired as CME during July 1946 and was succeeded by Arthur Peppercorn. Classified A2/3 by the LNER, No. 500 carried the name *Edward Thompson* and became No. 60500 with British Railways. Seen here bearing a 34E New England shed code, she would end her days allocated there until she was withdrawn in 1963. *Opposite*: Seen here at New England shed, Class B1 4-6-0 No. 61283 was constructed by the NBL and entered service during 1948. She is bearing a 31A Cambridge shed code and would see only fourteen years of service before being withdrawn in 1962.

Saturday 8 September 1962. This day saw the joint Stephenson Locomotive Society and Manchester Locomotive Society Leicestershire Railtour, which departed from Manchester Piccadilly station and travelled via Uttoxeter to Burton-on-Trent, where locomotives were changed. *Opposite*: Ex-LMS Class 5 2-6-0 'Crab' No. 42756 worked the train forward to Charnwood Forest Junction via Shakerstone Junction, and is seen here at Shakerstone. The design was attributed to George Hughes but was introduced in 1926 after Henry Fowler took over as CME. No. 42756 was constructed at Crewe Works during 1927 and would be withdrawn in 1964. *Right, top*: Ex-LMS Class 4F 0-6-0 No. 44109 then worked the train to Shepshed and back; seen here at Shepshed, No. 44109 was a product of Crewe Works during 1925 that would be withdrawn in 1964. *Right, bottom*: At Coalville a special run was made to Leicester West Bridge Goods Depot. Consisting of thirteen brake vans, the train was hauled by ex-MR Class '1142' (LMS Class 2F) 0-6-0 No. 58148. Seen here at West Bridge Goods Depot, No. 58148 was constructed by Beyer Peacock & Co. during 1876, and was withdrawn after eighty-seven years of service in 1963.

Sunday 2 June 1963. At Bingham station, ex-LNER Class B1 4-6-0 No. 61264 is at the head of a Nottingham Victoria to Mablethorpe special working. Constructed by the NBL in 1947 and allocated to Parkeston Quay to work the GE section, during 1960 she was transferred to Colwick shed in Nottinghamshire. Withdrawn in 1965 and transferred to service stock, she would become departmental No. 29 and utilised as a stationary boiler. Finally withdrawn from service during 1967 and sold to Woodham Brothers in Barry for scrap, she would be purchased by the Thompson B1 Locomotive Trust during the early 1970s and returned to steam during 1997. She is currently to be seen working at the North Yorkshire Moors Railway.

Sunday 2 June 1963. Class B1 4-6-0 No. 61299 is seen here on the approach to Bingham station with a special from Pleasley to Skegness. Constructed by the NBL during 1948, she would be withdrawn in 1965.